A Book of Pearls

Endorsements

Words can change worlds. So, feast on this compilation of quotes which have the potential to change how you see yourself and the world around you. An invaluable companion for life.
Professor Paul McGee - aka the SUMO Guy.

What an amazing collection Sue has put together. Every section gives you an aahh, wow or tear moment. I will cherish them and find a quote for every day. Thank you my friend.
Patti Hudspeth, Holistic health therapist and healer

Sue truly shows the tremendous power and influence words have over the human heart, mind, and soul. An excellently uplifting and re-readable book. Highly recommended.
Albie Gwen, Author: Pocket Brain

A Book of Pearls

Wise Quotes from all Ages

Sue Daly

Publications

Copyright

Dedication

Terry, my husband, for his love, support and patience on the path we walk together.

Our dear son ***Nicholas,*** for the Light and Hope he has brought to this life.

My parents ***Jim and Mary,*** for their love and wisdom in my upbringing.

My sister ***Penny****,* for always being there when I need her.

Contents

Alexander Inchbald

Foreword
Alexander Inchbald

"When sleeping women wake,
mountains move."
Chinese Proverb

W ise women are one of the most powerful forces in the world. After all, they have experienced so much life. They were born into a male dominated world, have given birth to life through them, brought up their children in a rapidly evolving environment, experienced love in all of its facets, come to terms with the constantly changing nature of their bodies and found a way to keep sharing from the heart, no matter what happens around them.

They may have played multiple different roles in life - inspirational leader, innovative creator, nurturing mother, dedicated partner, romantic lover and now, wise elder. What sets them apart though is their ability to contribute without an agenda, to influence without saying a word and yet, when needed to become a force of nature - the mysterious Shakti energy that comes from deep within and exposes the truth.

In ancient times, wise women were keepers of the primal mysteries and revered for these mystical powers.

Today, as we face some of the most pressing existential challenges humanity has ever seen, we need wise women more than ever. Many commentators have suggested the 21ˢᵗ Century is the century of women. I'm not so sure. Maybe our great grandchildren will look back on it and call it the century of wise women?

For the past 5,000 years, men have dominated the vast majority of human civilizations on this planet. And now, we find ourselves right at the edge of the precipice - with the climate crisis and inequality worsening. Men invented hierarchies, money, marriage and the measurement of time. In the first civilization in *Sumer* hierarchy created inequity between man and his fellow man. It placed one man above another, making those selected more important than the rest of us. Before that, each man had a role to play in the tribe or community. Hierarchies destroyed this sense of equality. Marriage made matters worse. It created a hierarchy between man and woman: the original marriage was designed so the man could guarantee 'his' woman was giving birth to 'his' child. It was a system of control that furthered inequity. Money and time are ways of measuring this inequity.

These four 'masculine' inventions created separation from our more feminine nature, from this deep Shakti energy and from Mother Nature. Wise women can help us reconnect to our feminine side, so we take more enlightened actions, before it's too late. Wise women can help us create a new, fairer, more humane world.

Sue Daly is a wise woman, who is helping us to do just this, elegantly and effortlessly. I first met Sue in a community of which we are both members. She attended a few complimentary sessions I was giving. I remember she rarely commented, but when she did, her comment was always insightful and struck a chord. What struck me even more was her presence, the energy that she embodied.

So, I was delighted when Sue agreed to join the *#Masterpiece ecosystem* which I founded, because I knew we would all benefit from her Masterpiece. And we do. Sue continues to share her pearls of wisdom with the rest of us.

What she has done in her Book of Pearls is an embodiment of who she is. She has gathered together and curated pearls of wisdom from authors, artists, leaders and visionaries into a clear narrative that speaks volumes about what she believes and who she is, without even writing a word.

This is the power of a wise woman—to influence everything without appearing to do anything.

Do not be deceived into thinking that all Sue has done is to put together a few quotes. This book is way more than that. It is the collective wisdom of humanity condensed into a few short pages.

Yes, many of these quotes are attributed to men. However, my research into the dynamics of creation reveals this wisdom comes from the feminine within us, the wise woman, if you like.

Imagine if every one of us embodied this wisdom - the climate crisis, war and inequity would end. We would experience heaven on earth. And yet, it's one thing to read a great quote. It's entirely another thing to live it every single day.

Imagine if you were to embody the wisdom in this book. After all, change starts with you. Your mindset influences your reality. Change your mindset and your reality changes.

So, rather than just reading these words and nodding in agreement, I invite you to reflect on them, consider why the original author wrote them or said them. And then, perhaps more importantly, consider why Sue included each pearl in her book, and in this order...

In other words, this isn't a book to read once. In fact, I'm not sure it's a book to read at all. I sense it's a book to keep close and, whenever you're struggling in life, to open it, find the relevant section and then a quote or an insight that will help.

This is what wise women do. Keep wise women close to you, even if you're not sure you need them at that moment, because you never know when life is going to change around you. And when it does, you may find they have exactly the pearl of wisdom you need.

In the meantime, I encourage you to dip into this Book of Pearls to see exactly what I mean.

With love

Alexander Inchbald,
Author of #Masterpiece

Introduction

Throughout the ages many words have been spoken. They were used to connect, encourage, inspire, amuse or express beliefs and emotions such as love, fear and hope. Some, passed on by word of mouth, became embedded in folklore and culture; and their exact origins are today unknown. Others were committed to the written word by their creators, and yet more recorded from speeches or presentations, some translated and adapted to suit a particular audience or purpose. Along the way, individuals may have claimed quotes or sayings for their own use, and the original source has become obscured.

For as long as I can remember I have collected quotations, poems and sayings which have touched me in some way or helped me better understand myself and this life I was born into. During the first coronavirus pandemic lockdown in 2020, I started to uncover and rediscover the many places where I had stored them, and realised how precious they were to me, for many different reasons.

Several people asked why I had chosen these particular quotations. In reality, they chose me, appearing serendipitously like a stranger who crosses your path and leaves an imprint on that particular moment in your life – or remains a friend forever. They came to me from diverse sources: my original Oxford Dictionary of Quotations gifted to me by friends of my parents, books I have read, conferences attended, inscriptions on walls and at exhibitions, greetings cards, songs, and more recently the internet and social media channels. For whatever reason, when the quotes appeared they struck a chord, shaping, supporting or occasionally challenging my values and beliefs. Now they remain woven into the tapestry of my personal lived experience.

I was also asked why I chose the sections into which they are arranged. This process evolved, and for convenience it seemed sensible to group the *pearls* into families. I recognise many of these wise words could sit in several of the sections, and *Love, Laughter, Connection, Learning and Growing* and *Overcoming* are all facets of humanity – being human. They may also point to our *Purpose* as we share *Our Natural World* with the other inhabitants of planet earth.

Every effort has been made to accurately trace the original source and wording of the quotes included, on the understanding that specific gender references were commonplace in their time, and if written today may be worded more inclusively.

We may not necessarily agree with what is being said, however we can reflect on the context and environment in which the words were originally used, to throw light on a different view of the world. For this reason, a reference of sources with brief background is included.

In addition, the book is designed for you to annotate and embellish with your own musings and drawings if you so choose, and to add your favourite quotations in the blank pages at the back of the book.

Are these *pearls* still relevant today, in a world which is very different from the time and place lived in by their originators? I leave it to you, my reader, to decide for yourself.

Enjoy!
Sue Daly

Laughter

Introducing Laughter

One of the most beautiful sounds in the world is the spontaneous laughter of young children: an expression of sheer delight at being alive and in the moment.

The physical, mental and emotional benefits of laughter are scientifically proven. Although I am unaware of any scientific measure of the spiritual benefits, I have observed those who find something to laugh about in the direst of circumstances appear to have an enhanced inner peace and strength.

I have often wondered if irony is God's idea of a joke, and he gave us a sense of humour so we could escape, momentarily, from the cares and worries of our everyday living - like the "birds of the air and the lilies of the field".

Have you ever stopped to wonder at when and why you laugh, and the impact it has on you and others?

Laughter is the shortest distance between two people.

Victor Borge

*What soap is to the body,
laughter is to the soul.*

Yiddish Proverb

A sense of humour... is needed armour.
Joy in one's heart and
some laughter on one's lips
is a sign that the person down deep
has a pretty good grasp of life.

Hugh Sidey

*We don't laugh
because we're happy,
we are happy
because we laugh.*

William James

*If you would not
be laughed at,
be the first to
laugh at yourself.*

Benjamin Franklin

*A good laugh is
sunshine in the house.*

William Thackeray

*Life does not cease to be
funny when people die
any more than it ceases to be
serious when people laugh.*

George Bernard Shaw

*A smile starts on the lips,
a grin spreads to the eyes,
a chuckle comes from the belly;
but a good laugh bursts forth
from the soul, overflows, and
bubbles all around.*

Carolyn Birmingham

10

*You don't stop laughing
because you grow old.
You grow old because
you stop laughing.*

Michael Pritchard

*To truly laugh, you must
be able to take your pain and play with it.*

Charlie Chaplin

*Laughter is the sun
that drives winter
from the human face.*

Victor Hugo

A good laugh heals a lot of hurts.

Madeleine L'Engle

*I have not seen anyone
dying of laughter,
but I know millions
who are dying because
they are not laughing.*

Dr. Madan Kataria

*Life is too important to
be taken seriously.*

Oscar Wilde

Love

Introducing Love

There are many different manifestations of love: great works of art have been inspired by it; we will do for love what we would not do for money or any other reward. It can be all consuming, we will make sacrifices, travel great distances, be prepared to appear foolish, and so the list goes on. Without love we feel empty, disconnected and without purpose.

How does love appear in your life? Are you aware of how many times in a day you experience the giving or receiving of love, in any of its different forms?

That love is all there is,
is all we know of love.

Emily Dickinson

*Love possesses not nor
would it be possessed.*

Kahlil Gibran

This morning I will not comb my hair; it has lain pillowed on the hand of my lover.

Kakinomoto no Hitomaro

If you love something,
set it free.
If it comes back,
it is yours.
If it doesn't, it never was.

Unknown

*Passion makes the
world go 'round.
Love just makes
it a safer place.*

Tracy Lauren Marrow

*In order to create
there must be a dynamic force,
and what force is more
potent than love?*

Igor Stravinsky

He who binds to himself a joy,
Does the winged life destroy,
He who kisses the joy as it flies,
Lives in eternity's sunrise.

William Blake

*Loving is not just
caring deeply,
it's, above all,
understanding.*

Françoise Sagan

*A heart is not judged
by how much you love;
but by how much you are
loved by others.*

L Frank Baum

Where there is great love, there are always miracles.

Willa Cather

*Grief is the price
we pay for love.*

Queen Elizabeth II

Love is the whole thing.
We are only pieces.

Rumi

*Your love is your greatest
gift to the world.*

Alexander Inchbald

You can't blame gravity
for falling in love.

Albert Einstein

*Give your hearts, but not
into each other's keeping.
For only the hand of Life
can contain your hearts.
And stand together yet not
too near together; for the pillars
of the temple stand apart, and
the oak tree and the cypress grow
not in each other's shadow.*

Kahlil Gibran

*Love makes your soul crawl
out from its hiding place.*

Zora Neale Hurston

*The greatest healing therapy
is friendship and love.*

Hubert H Humphrey

You will find as you look back upon your life that the moments when you have truly lived are the moments when you have done things in the spirit of love. To love abundantly is to live abundantly, and to love forever is to live forever.

Henry Drummond

Namaste

I honour the place in you where the entire universe resides.
I honour the place in you of love, of truth, of peace and of light, and when you are in that place in you and I am in that place in me, there is only one of us.

Hindu Greeting

*When you go out and see
the empty streets,*

*the empty stadiums, the
empty train platforms,*

*don't say to yourself,
"It looks like the end of the world."*

What you're seeing is love in action.

*What you're seeing, in that
negative space, is how much
we do care for each other,*

*for our grandparents,
our parents,
our brothers and sisters,
for people we will never meet.*

People will lose jobs over this.

Some will lose their businesses.

And some will lose their lives.

All the more reason to take a moment,
when you're out on your walk,
or on your way to the store,
or just watching the news,
to look into the emptiness and
marvel at all of that love.

Let it fill you and sustain you.

It isn't the end of the world.

It is the most remarkable act of global
solidarity we may ever witness.

Belfast COVID Team, 2020

Time flies
Sunrise and shadow fall
Love is forever
Over all.

Unknown

Connection

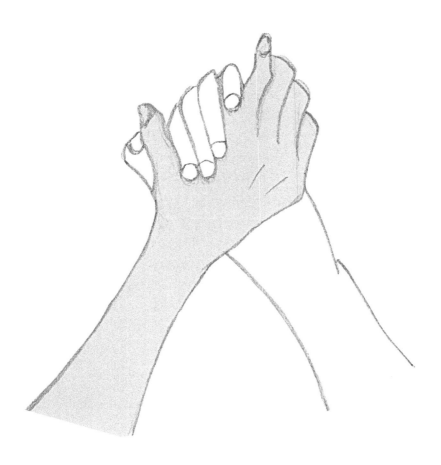

Introducing Connection

In our quiet moments, alone, we may feel connected with our environment, nature, or the divinity of our belief system. The *pearls* in this section focus on our relationships with other human beings; how we communicate, and how our relationship with ourself impacts on our relationships with others.

The ideas here are reflected in all work relating to the better functioning of teams, groups and societies. They come back, full circle, to us as individuals having a richer and more fulfilling experience as members of those collectives.

*Many people will walk in
and out of your life, but only true friends
will leave footprints in your heart.*

Eleanor Roosevelt

*Seek first to understand,
then to be understood.*

Stephen Covey

The road to a friend's house is never long.

Danish Proverb

True happiness consists not in the multitude of friends, but in their worth and choice.

Ben Jonson

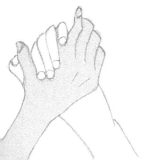

The ideas that have lighted my way and, time after time, have given me new courage to face life cheerfully have been Kindness, Beauty, and Truth.

Albert Einstein

*I'm always amazed
how readily people judge the
right and wrong of things they
know only from the outside.*

David Clawson

*Resentment is like
drinking poison and then
hoping it will kill your enemies.*

Nelson Mandela

*We judge ourselves
by our intentions;
others judge us
by our behaviours.*

Carl Jung

What other people think of you really isn't any of your business: it's best to not let other people's opinions prevent you from being the authentic version of yourself.

Sonia Vadlamani

*Be who you are and
say what you feel because...
Those who mind don't matter
and those who matter don't mind*

Theodore Geisel (Dr Seuss)

*Some people will never like you
because your spirit
irritates their demons.*

Denzel Washington

The only way to change someone's mind is to connect with them from the heart.

Rasheed Ogunlaru

Nobody can make you feel inferior without your consent.

Eleanor Roosevelt

*Example is not the main thing
in influencing others,
it is the only thing.*

Albert Schweitzer

*If there is any great secret
of success in life,
it lies in the ability
to put yourself in the other
person's place and to see things from
his point of view – as well as your own.*

Henry Ford

*Am I not destroying my enemies
when I make friends of them?*

Abraham Lincoln

Life becomes easier when you learn to accept the apology you never got.

Robert Brault

*No one will ever win
the battle of the sexes;
there's too much
fraternising with the enemy.*

Henry Kissinger

*I've learned that people
will forget what you said,
people will forget what you did,
but people will never forget
how you made them feel.*

Maya Angelou

*Empathy is
simply listening,
holding space,
withholding judgment,
emotionally connecting, and
communicating that
incredibly healing
message of you're not alone.*

Brené Brown

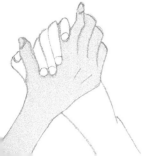

The moment we become upset with someone it means we are trying to control them.

Mike George

*When you finally learn
a person's behaviour has more
to do with their internal struggle
than ever it did with you...
you learn grace.*

Allison Aars

*Weak minds compete,
great minds collaborate.*

Markus Cox

*A leader does not deserve
the name unless he is willing
occasionally to stand alone.*

Henry Kissinger

This is a story about four people named Everybody, Somebody, Anybody and Nobody.

There was an important job to be done and Everybody was sure that Somebody would do it.

Anybody could have done it, but Nobody did it.

Somebody got angry about that, because it was Everybody's job.

Everybody thought Anybody could do it, but Nobody realised Everybody wouldn't do it.

It ended up that Everybody blamed Somebody when Nobody did what Anybody could have!

Charles Osgood

*Independence?
That's middle class blasphemy.
We are all dependent
on one another,
every soul of us on earth.*

George Bernard Shaw

If you want to go fast, go alone;
if you want to go far, go together.

African Proverb

*Under the shelter of
each other, people survive.*

Unknown

*Treat yourself well
and cherish others.*

Paul McGee

71

*We shall never know
all the good that a
simple smile can do.*

Mother Teresa

*Only when human beings
are able to perceive and
acknowledge the Self in each
other can there be real peace.*

Mata Amritanandamayi

Life I touch for good or ill will touch another life, and in turn another, until who knows where the trembling stops or in what far place my touch will be felt.

Frederick Buechner

Purpose

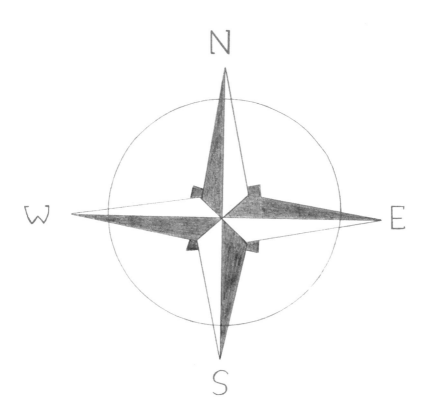

Introducing Purpose

What's the point of this? Purpose forms part of many motivational theories: it sits at the top of *Abraham Maslow's,* Hierarchy of Needs as Self-actualisation – becoming all we were intended to be. It is also one of *Daniel Pink's* three motivational factors for 21st century work, along with Autonomy and Mastery.

"Why am I here?" is an existential question to which we may never discover the answer until looking back from the end of our life. Yet in one lifetime there are many moments, and every single word or deed will send out ripples to the wider environment; we may never know the end consequences, good or bad.

So, perhaps it is better to ask, "What is my intention?" If we care to consider our intent in each moment as we live it, then perhaps the ultimate purpose of our whole life will become clearer to us.

Learn to get in touch with the silence within yourself and know that everything in this life has a purpose.

Elisabeth Kubler-Ross

A ship in port is safe,
but that's not what
ships are built for.

Grace Hopper

*It's your road and yours alone.
Others may walk it with you, but
no one can walk it for you.*

Rumi

Our freedom, peace, and joy in the present moment is the most important thing we have.

Thích Nhất Hạnh

*Your time is limited,
so don't waste it living
someone else's life.
Don't be trapped by dogma –
which is living with the results of
other people's thinking.
Don't let the noise of others'
opinions drown out
your own inner voice.
And most importantly,
have the courage to follow
your heart and intuition.
They somehow already know
what you truly want to become.
Everything else is secondary.*

Steve Jobs

*The most creative act you will
ever undertake is the act
of creating yourself.*

Deepak Chopra

*If you don't know
where you are going,
every road will
get you nowhere.*

Henry Kissinger

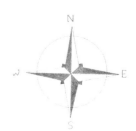

*Watch your thoughts;
they become words.*

*Watch your words;
they become actions.*

*Watch your actions;
they become habits.*

*Watch your habits;
they become character.*

*Watch your character;
it becomes your destiny.*

Lao Tzu

Get a lot of sleep,
a lot of exercise.
Eat real good.
Say your prayers.
And be good to your dogs.

Mickey Rourke

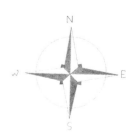

Once upon a time an old man was walking along the shore after a big storm had passed and found the beach littered with starfish as far as the eye could see, stretching in both directions.

In the distance the old man noticed a small boy approaching. As the boy walked, he paused every so often and as he grew closer the man could see that the boy was occasionally bending down to pick up an object and throw it into the sea. The boy came closer still and the man called out, "Good morning! May I ask what you are doing?"

The young boy paused, looked up and replied, "Throwing starfish into the ocean. The tide has washed them up

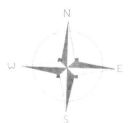

onto the beach and they can't return to the sea by themselves. When the sun gets high they will die unless I throw them back into the water."

The old man replied, "But there must be tens of thousands of starfish on this beach. I'm afraid you won't really be able to make much of a difference."

The boy bent down, picked up yet another starfish and threw it as far as he could into the ocean. He turned, smiled and said,
"I made a difference for that one"

Loren Eiseley
Adapted: The Star Thrower

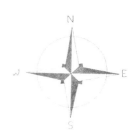

Measure your self-worth not with the balance of your bank account but with the frequency of your generosity.

Haemin Sunim

*Things which matter most
must never be at the
mercy of things
which matter least.*

Johann Wolfgang Goethe

I am in competition with no-one.
I have no desire to play the game
of being better than anyone.
I am simply trying to be better
than the person I was yesterday.

Unknown

*What lies behind us and
what lies before us
are tiny matters compared
to what lies within us.*

Ralph Waldo Emerson

*We are here to awaken
from our illusion
of separateness.*

Thích Nhất Hạnh

I believe you have been born into this time because you have a role to play in the future of humanity. But all that starts with a deeper understanding of what is really going on.

Nicholas Haines

*True purpose is found in giving
yourself one hundred percent to
every moment, rather than having
to do with any kind of achievement.*

Richard Rudd

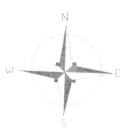

Integrity is not exercised in words, it is lived in deeds.

Unknown

There is no need for temples.
No need for complicated philosophies.
My brain and my heart
are my temples;
My philosophy is kindness.

Tenzin Gyatso
14th Dalai Lama

*Your talent is
God's gift to you.
What you do with it is
your gift back to God.*

Leo Buscaglia

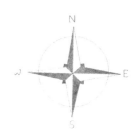

If there is light in the soul,
There will be beauty in the person.
If there is beauty in the person,
There will be harmony in the house.
If there is harmony in the house,
There will be order in the nation.
If there is order in the nation,
There will be peace in the world.

Chinese Proverb

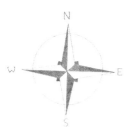

*If you have built your
castles in the air,
your work need not be lost.
That is where they should be.
Now, put the foundations under them.*

Henry David Thoreau

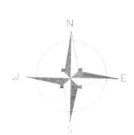

The things you do for
yourself are gone when
you are gone, but the things you do
for others remain as your legacy.

Kalu Ndukwe Kalu

*Heaven is a palace
with many doors, and each
may enter in his own way.*

Hindu Saying

When I stand before God
at the end of my life, I would
hope that I would not have a single
bit of talent left, that I could say,
"I used everything you gave me."

Erma Bombeck

Humanity

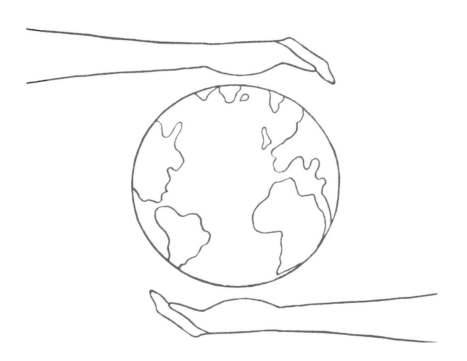

Introducing
Humanity

This collection of quotes explores our personal motivations and beliefs. It serves as a reminder of our ability, as humans, to take control of our thoughts to make the best of our human experience. In doing so, we can also create a more harmonious world for all inhabitants of planet earth, as referred to in Phyllis Schlemmer's book, *The Only Planet of Choice*.

*There is more wisdom
in your body than in your
deepest philosophies.*

Friedrich Nietzsche

*He has the most
who is most content
with the least.*

Diogenes

*In three words
I can sum up everything
I've learned about life:
it goes on.*

Robert Frost

*I am who I am today
because of the choices
I made yesterday.*

Stephen Covey

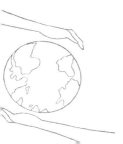

*If you want to know
who is most responsible
for where you are in life,
take a look in the mirror.*

Paul McGee

*There is nothing
either good or bad,
but thinking makes it so.*

William Shakespeare

*Whether you think you can,
or you think you can't
– you're right.*

Henry Ford

*My experiences in the past
have not made me the way I am;
my experiences in the past
have made me believe
I am the way I am.*

Skip Ross

*Honesty is commended,
and starves.*

Juvenal

Only put off until tomorrow what you are willing to die having left undone.

Pablo Picasso

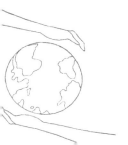

Done is better than perfect.

Sheryl Sandberg

People tend to overestimate what they can achieve in a year, but underestimate what they can achieve in a lifetime.

Anthony Robbins

*Here's the thing about beliefs:
they don't have to be true
to be powerful.*

Paul McGee

Holding on to anything
is like holding on to your breath.
You will suffocate.
The only way to get anything
in the physical universe is
by letting go of it.
Let go and
it will be yours forever.

Deepak Chopra

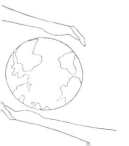

Ability is what you're capable of doing. Motivation determines what you do. Attitude determines how well you do it.

Lou Holtz

It's better to have a mind opened by wonder than a mind closed by belief.

Gerry Spence

Do not apologize for crying.
Without this emotion,
we are only robots.

Elizabeth Gilbert

*There is very little
difference in people.
But that little difference
makes a big difference.
The little difference is attitude.
The big difference is whether
it is positive or negative.*

W Clement Stone

*The day she let go of the things
that were weighing her down,
was the day she began
to shine the brightest.*

Katrina Mayer

*Human beings, by changing
the inner attitudes of their minds,
can change the outer aspects of their lives.*

William James

124

*Change the way
you look at things
and the things
you look at change.*

Wayne Dyer

*The only thing worse
than being blind
is having sight
but no vision.*

Helen Keller

*It's time we learned
this world was made
for all men.*

Stevie Wonder

*People with clear, written goals
accomplish far more
in a shorter period of time
than people without them
could ever imagine.*

Brian Tracy

*Motivation is a fire from within.
If someone else tries to light that fire under
you, chances are it will burn very briefly.*

Steven Covey

Commitment is doing the thing you said you were going to do long after the mood you said it in has left you.

Darren Hardy

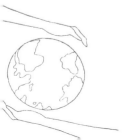

*For your own emotional wellbeing,
please resign from being
General Manager of the universe.
Relaxing and resting are not
sackable offences.*

Paul McGee

Never try to teach a pig to sing;
it wastes your time
and it annoys the pig.

Robert Heinlein

*Everyone who has ever
taken a shower has had an idea.
It's the person who gets out of the
shower, dries off, and does something
about it that makes a difference.*

Nolan Bushnell

*It's not that some people
have willpower and some don't.
It's that some people are ready to
change and others are not.*

James Gordon

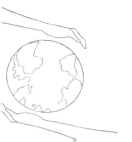

134

*Great things are done
by a series of small
things brought together.*

Vincent Van Gogh

Sometimes the most important thing in a whole day is the rest we take between two deep breaths.

Etty Hillesum

*There is nothing so useless
as doing efficiently that which
should not be done at all.*

Peter Drucker

The more I practise,
the luckier I get.

Gary Player

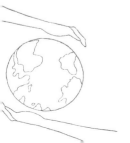

Are you in earnest?
Seize this very minute;

What you can do, or dream
you can, begin it;

Boldness has genius, power
and magic in it.

Only engage, and then the
mind grows heated;

Begin, and then the work
will be completed.

Johann Wolfgang Goethe

Beginning is half done.

Robert H Schuller

*Abundance is our natural state.
It doesn't always feel that way,
especially when we're surrounded
by poverty, disease, and conflict.*

*The trick lies in welcoming whatever
emotion is here, letting it grow, embracing
it with our love, and allowing it to move
through us until there is nothing left.
That's how we find peace within ourselves.*

*And it's from within that space of
peace where healing begins.*

Allison Ross

*We consume social media
to affirm not to inform our beliefs.*

Daniel Lubetsky

*We do not need magic
to transform our world.
We carry all of the power we need
inside ourselves already.*

J K Rowling

Men occasionally stumble over the truth, but most of them pick themselves up and hurry off as if nothing happened.

Winston Churchill

When sleeping women wake,
mountains move.

Chinese Proverb

Learning and
Growing

Introducing Learning and Growing

We live in an age of information (and sometimes disinformation), so opportunities to learn new things have never been more plentiful, and often overwhelming.

If we look at nature, there is no such thing as standing still; living organisms are always growing and/or changing. Our challenge can be, as the world around us changes, we are reluctant to let go of older ideas, which may have become rigid beliefs, to make room for new and more relevant learnings.

No one person can 'know' absolutely everything there is to know on this earth; it is enough to learn the lessons our own life experiences afford us.

Teachers open the door,
but you must enter by yourself.

Chinese Proverb

Begin with the end in mind.

Steven Covey

*Set a goal so big that
you can't achieve it until you
grow into the person who can.*

Zig Ziglar

*All our knowledge is
ourselves to know.*

Alexander Pope

*Your body hears everything
your mind says.*

Naomi Judd

*If we don't change,
we don't grow,
and if we don't grow,
we are not really living.*

Gail Sheehy

*Education is the
most powerful weapon which
you can use to change the world.*

Nelson Mandela

*Anyone who stops learning is old,
whether at twenty or eighty.*

Henry Ford

The mind, once stretched by a new idea, never returns to its original dimensions.

Ralph Waldo Emerson

Old ways won't open new doors.

Proverb

Has your comfort blanket actually become your straitjacket?

Paul McGee

Progress is impossible without change, and those who cannot change their minds cannot change anything.

George Bernard Shaw

*No problem can be solved
from the same level
of consciousness
that created it.*

Albert Einstein

*He who stops being better
stops being good.*

Oliver Cromwell

*We could never learn
to be brave and patient,
if there were only joy in the world.*

Helen Keller

The hardest job is teaching children good manners when they don't see any.

Fred Astaire

*First and foremost,
we need to be the adults
we want our children to be.
We should watch our own
gossiping and anger.
We should model the kindness
we want to see.*

Brené Brown

*If you want to see
what children can do,
you must stop giving them things.*

Norman Douglas

*Investing in yourself
is the best investment
you will ever make.
It will not only improve your life,
it will improve the lives of
all those around you.*

Robin Sharma

*Where is the wisdom
we have lost in knowledge?
Where is the knowledge we
have lost in information?*

T. S. Eliot

Every man gets a narrower and narrower field of knowledge in which he must be an expert in order to compete with other people. The specialist knows more and more about less and less and finally knows everything about nothing.

Konrad Lorenz

*When you talk,
you are only repeating
what you already know.
But if you listen, you may
learn something new.*

**Tenzin Gyatso
14th Dalai Lama**

*If you never
change your mind,
why have one?*

Edward de Bono

*When a man gives himself
totally to fixed ideas
he is destroyed by them.*

Honoré de Balzac

*The people who enrich their minds
are those who keep their history
on the leaves of memory.*

Glenn H Welker

*A mentor is not someone
who walks ahead of us
to show us how they did it.
A mentor walks alongside us
to show us what we can do.*

Simon Sinek

*Everything that irritates
us about others
can lead us to a better
understanding of ourselves.*

Carl Jung

*Anger makes you smaller,
while forgiveness forces you to
grow beyond what you were.*

Cherie Carter-Scott

The illiterate of the 21ˢᵗ century will not be those who cannot read and write, but those who cannot learn, unlearn, and relearn.

Alvin Toffler

Deconstruction creates knowledge.
Recombination creates value.

James Clear

If you want one year of prosperity, grow seeds.

If you want ten years of prosperity, grow trees.

If you want a lifetime of prosperity, grow people.

Chinese Proverb

*Change will not come
if we wait for some other
person or some other time.
We are the ones
we've been waiting for.
We are the change that we seek.*

Barack Obama

*Everyone thinks of
changing the world,
but no one thinks
of changing himself.*

Leo Tolstoy

Autobiography in five short chapters

I

I walk down the street.
There is a deep hole in the sidewalk.
I fall in.
I am lost ... I am helpless.
It isn't my fault.
It takes me forever to find a way out.

II

I walk down the same street.
There is a deep hole in the sidewalk.
I pretend I don't see it.
I fall in again.
I can't believe I am in the same place.
But it isn't my fault.
It still takes a long time to get out.

III
I walk down the same street.
There is a deep hole in the sidewalk.
I see it is there.
I still fall in ... it's a habit.
My eyes are open.
I know where I am.
It is my fault.
I get out immediately.

IV
I walk down the same street.
There is a deep hole in the sidewalk.
I walk around it.

V
I walk down another street.

Portia Nelson

*Between stimulus and response
there is a space.
In that space is our power
to choose our response.
In our response lies our
growth and our freedom.*

Viktor E Frankl

Overcoming

Introducing
Overcoming

U ndoubtedly life's greatest lessons come from the experiences which challenge us the most.

Of all the quotations in this book, those in this section are the ones I turn to most: to remind me to be grateful not to have endured such extreme challenges as many others have, and to reassure me if ever I do, I will somehow be equipped to deal with them.

Remember who you were before you were born, and you will never know fear.

Unknown

*It is not because
things are difficult
that we do not dare;
it is because we do not dare
that they are difficult.*

Seneca

*He who has a 'why'
to live can bear
almost any 'how'.*

Viktor E Frankl

You never know how strong you are until being strong is the only choice you have.

Unknown

Courage is grace under pressure.

Ernest Hemingway

*If you're going through hell,
keep going.*

Winston Churchill

Sorrow prepares you for joy.
It violently sweeps everything
out of your house,
so that new joy can find
space to enter.
It shakes the yellow leaves
from the bough of your heart,
so that fresh, green leaves
can grow in their place.
It pulls up the rotten roots,
so that new roots hidden
beneath have room to grow.
Whatever sorrow shakes
from your heart,
far better things will
take their place.

Rumi

Tough times never last, tough people do.

Robert H Schuller

*You can't stop the waves
but you can learn to surf.*

Jon Kabat-Zinn

The worst times make for the greatest opportunities.

Roger Fritz

Success is not final,
failure is not fatal:
it is the courage to
continue that counts.

Winston Churchill

*Effort only fully releases
its reward after a person
refuses to quit.*

Napoleon Hill

People are always blaming their circumstances for what they are. I don't believe in circumstances. The people who get on in the world are the people who get up and look for the circumstances they want, and if they can't find them, make them.

George Bernard Shaw

*The best way out
is always through.*

Robert Frost

*You know when great things
are coming when everything
seems to be going wrong.
Old energy is clearing out
for new energy to enter.
Be patient.*

Idil Ahmed

*Every adversity,
every failure,
and every heartache
carries with it the seed of an
equivalent or greater benefit.*

Napoleon Hill

*If you are not happy
with the answers
life is giving you,
then ask some
different questions.*

Paul McGee

*Fear is a reaction,
courage is a choice.*
Winston Churchill

*People who say,
"It cannot be done"
should not interrupt
those who are doing it.*

Chinese Proverb

The only thing necessary for the triumph of evil is for good men to do nothing.

Edmund Burke

*Cowardice asks the
question: "Is it safe?"*

*Expediency asks the
question: "Is it politic?"*

*Vanity asks the
question: "Is it popular?"*

*But conscience asks the
question: "Is it right?"*

*And there comes a time
when one must take
a position that is neither
safe, nor politic, nor popular
– but one must take it simply
because it is right.*

Dr Martin Luther King Jnr

*Everything can be taken
from a man but one thing:
the last of human freedoms
- to choose one's attitude in
any given set of circumstances,
to choose one's own way.*

Viktor E Frankl

The will must be greater than the skill.

Muhammad Ali

*Those who would give up
essential Liberty, to purchase
a little temporary Safety,
deserve neither
Liberty nor Safety.*

Benjamin Franklin

*Let your hopes,
not your hurts,
shape your future.*

Robert Schuller

In the midst of movement and chaos, keep stillness inside of you.

Deepak Chopra

Never, never, never give up.

Winston Churchill

Our Natural World

Introducing
Our Natural World

If ever you watch small children left to their own devices in a garden, park or other green space, you will notice their total concentration and wonderment as they explore every leaf, plant, insect or flower.

We cannot isolate ourselves from the natural world; this planet and every aspect of nature is crucial to our survival as a species here.

We are at a tipping point in realising we cannot continue to exploit earth's resources, destroy habitats, and eliminate other species in order to satisfy our own desires.

May we all count our blessings and return to that childlike wonder and respect for Mother Nature - our Natural World.

Look deep into nature,
and then you will
understand everything better.

Albert Einstein

Treat the earth well:
it was not given to you
by your parents,
it was loaned to you
by your children.

Thasunke Witko
Crazy Horse

To see a World in a Grain of Sand
And a Heaven in a Wild Flower
Hold Infinity in the palm of your hand
And Eternity in an hour.

William Blake

*Nature does not hurry
yet everything
is accomplished.*

Lao Tzu

Earth laughs in flowers.
Ralph Waldo Emerson

*Man does not weave
this web of life,
he is merely a strand in it.
Whatever he does to the
web he does to himself.*

Chief Seattle Sealth

When the sun rises,
it rises for everyone.

Cuban Proverb

*No bird soars too high
if he soars with
his own wings.*

William Blake

*When you realise
nothing is lacking,
the whole world
belongs to you.*

Lao Tzu

Take care of your body.
It's the only place
you have to live in.

Jim Rohn

*Just when the caterpillar
thought the world was over,
it became a butterfly.*

Chuang Tzu

One drop raises the ocean.
Arthur Conan Doyle

*It is not the strongest
of the species that survive,
nor the most intelligent,
but the ones most
responsive to change.*

Charles Darwin

*Only after the last tree
has been cut down*

*Only after the last river
has been poisoned*

*Only after the last fish
has been caught*

*Then will you find that
money cannot be eaten.*

Cree Prophecy

*Men go abroad to wonder
at the heights of mountains,*

*at the huge waves of the sea,
at the long courses of the rivers,*

*at the vast compass of the ocean,
at the circular motions of*

*the stars, and they pass by
themselves without wondering.*

Saint Augustine

References

Introduction

Matthew 6:26-28, *English Standard version of the New Testament*, (William Collins), 2017.

Love

Gibran, Kalil, The Prophet, (Pan Books), 1991.

Windsor, Elizabeth, following the September 11 attacks in New York, 2021

Connection

Vadlamani, Sonia, *What Other People Think of You is None of Your Business*, (Happiness.com online magazine), https://www.happiness.com/magazine/personal-growth/what-other-people-think-of-you-is-none-of-your-business/, 02/02/2022.

Purpose

Eiseley, Loren, *adapted from 'The Star Thrower' first published 1969 in 'The Unexpected Universe' and republished 1978 in a collection of stories under the name 'The Star Thrower'.*

Hahn, Thich Nhat, *No Death, No Fear*, (Rider), 2002.

Maslow, Abraham, *A Theory of Human Motivation*, (Psychological Review Journal), 1943.

Pink, Daniel, *Drive*, (Canongate Books Ltd), 2009.

Rourke, Mickey, *Time Magazine Feb 9 2009*,
Jose G. Camil of Queretaro, Mexico,
https://www.joanborysenko.com/wp-content/uploads/
Resilience-article-book-excerpt.pdf, 02/02/2022.

Humanity

Schlemmer, Phyllis, edited by Jenkins, Palden, *The Only
Planet of Choice: Essential Briefings from Deep Space*,
(Gateway), 1996.

Shakespeare, William, Hamlet, Act 2 Scene 2.

Wonder, Stevie, *Black Man*, (Tamla Records), LP/
CD, Album: Songs in the Key of Life, 1976.

Learning and Growing

Sheehy, Gail, *Passages: Predictable Crises
of Adult Life*, (Ballantine Books), 2006.

Overcoming

Fritz, Roger, *The Power of a Positive Attitude:
Discovering the Key to Success*, (AMACOM), 2008.

Our Natural World

Blake, William and Jonson, Will, *Auguries of Innocence
and other Lyric Poems*, (CreateSpace), 2014.

Doyle, Arthur Conan, *The Lost World*, Director:
Orme, Stuart, BBC, RTL, A&E Network, 2001.

List of Quotees

Aars, Allison (1980 -) American entrepreneur.

Ahmed, Idil (Dates unknown) American author, speaker.

Ali, Muhammad (1942 - 2016) American professional boxer, activist.

Amritanandamayi, Mata (Amma) (1953 -) Indian Hindu spiritual leader, humanitarian.

Angelou, Maya (1928 - 2014) American poet, activist.

Astaire, Fred (1899 - 1987) American actor, dancer, singer.

Augustine, Saint (354 - 430) Roman Berber theologian, philosopher.

Baum, Lyman Frank (1856 - 1919) American author, Wizard of Oz.

Birmingham, Carolyn (1964 -) American recreation educator.

Blake, William (1757 - 1827) English poet, painter.

Bombeck, Erma (1927 - 1996) American humorist, writer.

Borge, Victor (1909 - 2000) Danish entertainer.

Brault, Robert (1938 -) American freelance writer.

Brown, Brené (1965 -) American professor, author.

Buechner, Frederick (1926 - 2022) American writer, preacher, theologian.

Burke, Edmund (1729 - 1797, British statesman, economist, philosopher.

Buscaglia, Leo 1924 - 1998) American author, motivational speaker, educator.

Bushnell, Nolan (1943 -) American businessman, electrical engineer.

Carter-Scott, Cherie (1949 -) American author, coach.

Cather, Willa (1873 - 1947) American writer, novelist.

Chaplin, Charlie (1889 - 1977) British actor, comedian, film director/producer.

Chopra, Deepak (1946 -) Indian American author, speaker.

Churchill, Winston (1874 - 1965) British politician, UK Prime Minister from 1940 to 1945 and 1951 to 1955.

Clawson, David (1967 -) American football coach.

Clear, James (1986 -) American author, entrepreneur, photographer.

Covey, Stephen (1932 - 2012) American author, educator, businessman.

Cox, Markus (1976 -) British property developer.

Cromwell, Oliver (1599 - 1658) English general, statesman, Lord Protector from 1653 to 1658.

Darwin, Charles (1809 - 1882) English naturalist, geologist, biologist.

Daskall, Lolly (Dates unknown) American speaker, coach, author.

de Balzac, Honoré (1799 - 1850) French writer, journalist.

de Bono, Edward (1933 - 2021) British Maltese psychologist, author.

Dickinson, Emily (1830 - 1886) American poet.

Diogenes, Laertius (412 BC - 323 BC) Greek philosopher.

Douglas, Norman (1868 - 1952) British author.

Doyle, Arthur Conan (1859 - 1930) British author, physician.

Drummond, Henry (1851 - 1897) Scottish biologist, author, evangelist.

Drucker, Peter (1909 - 2005) Austrian-American management consultant, author.

Dyer, Wayne (1940 - 2015) American author, speaker.

Einstein, Albert (1879 - 1955) American theoretical physicist of German-Swiss origin.

Eiseley, Loren (1907 - 1977) American anthropologist, author.

Eliot, T. S (1888 - 1965) British poet, playwright.

Emerson, Ralph Waldo (1803 - 1882) American essayist, poet.

Ford, Henry (1863 - 1947) American industrialist, business magnate.

Frankl, Viktor, E (1905 - 1997) Austrian psychiatrist, philosopher, holocaust survivor.

Franklin, Benjamin (1706 - 1790) American polymath, Founding Father of the United States.

Fritz, Roger (1928 - 2011) American consultant, author.

Frost, Robert (1874 - 1963) American poet.

Gandhi, Mahatma (1869 - 1948) Indian lawyer, nationalist.

Geisel, Theodore aka Dr Seuss, (1904 - 1991) American children's author.

George, Mike (Dates unknown) British author, speaker, spiritual coach.

Gibran, Kahlil (1883 - 1931) Lebanese-American writer, artist.

Gilbert, Elizabeth (1969 -) American journalist, novelist.

Goethe, Johann Wolfgang (1749 - 1832) German writer, scientist, critic.

Gordon, James (1966 -) Canadian singer-songwriter.

Gyatso, Tenzin, (1935 -) 14th Dalai Lama, Tibetan Buddhist leader.

Haines, Nicholas (1959 -) British author, Kindness Ambassador, creator of the Vitality Test.

Hanh, Thich Nhat (1926 - 2022) Vietnamese Buddhist monk, peace activist.

Hardy, Darren (1971 -) American author, speaker, publisher.

Heinlein, Robert (1907 - 1988) American author, aeronautical engineer, naval officer.

Hemingway, Ernest (1899 - 1961) American author, novelist.

Hill, Napoleon (1883 - 1970) American self-help author.

Hillesum, Etty (1914 - 1943) Dutch author.

Holtz, Lou (1935 -) American footballer, coach.

Hopper, Grace (1906 - 1992) American computer scientist, Navy Rear Admiral.

Hugo, Victor (1802 - 1885) French poet, novelist.

Humphrey, Hubert H (1911 - 1978) American politician, Vice president from 1965 to 1969.

Hurston, Zora Neale (1891 - 1960) American author, anthropologist, film maker.

Inchbald, Alexander (1974 -) British extreme artist, author, founder of Masterpiece Ecosystem.

James, William (1842 - 1910) American philosopher, historian, psychologist

Jobs, Steve (1955 - 2011) American business magnate, co-founder of Apple Inc.

Jonson, Ben (1572 - 1637) English playwright, poet.

Judd, Naomi (1946 - 2022) American singer-songwriter, actress.

Jung, Carl (1875 - 1961) Swiss psychiatrist, psychoanalyst.

Juvenal, Decimus Junius (55 AD - Date unknown) Roman satirical poet.

Kabat-Zinn, Jon (1944 -) American professor, founder of mindfulness-based stress reduction.

Kakinomoto, Hitomaro (650 - 710) Japanese poet, aristocrat.

Kalu, Kalu Ndukwe (Dates unknown) Nigerian-American political scientist, author.

Kataria, Madan (1955 -) Indian motivational speaker, founder of laughter yoga.

Keller, Helen (1880 - 1968) American author, lecturer, political activist.

King, Martin Luther Jnr (1929 - 1968) American Baptist minister, activist.

Kipling, Rudyard (1865 - 1936) English journalist, author, poet.

Kissinger, Henry (1923 -) American politician, diplomat.

Kubler-Ross, Elizabeth (1926 - 2004) Swiss-American psychiatrist, author.

L'Engle, Madeleine (1918 - 2007) American author.

Lincoln, Abraham (1809 - 1865) American lawyer, statesman, US president from 1861 to 1865.

Lorenz, Konrad (1903 - 1989) Austrian zoologist, ethologist.

Lubetzky, Daniel (1968 -) Mexican businessman, philanthropist, author.

Mandela, Nelson (1918 - 2013) philanthropist, President of South Africa from 1994 to 1999.

Marrow, Tracy Lauren aka Ice-T (1958 -) American rapper, songwriter, actor.

Maslow, Abraham (1908 - 1970) American psychologist, author, creator of his hierarchy of needs.

Mayer, Katrina (Dates unknown) American author, workshop leader.

McGee, Paul aka SUMO Guy (1964 -) British author, motivational speaker.

Mother Teresa (1910 - 1997) Albanian-Indian nun and missionary, beatified in 2003 as St Teresa of Calcutta.

Nelson, Portia (1920 - 2001) American singer-songwriter, author.

Nietzsche, Friedrich (1844 - 1900) German philosopher, essayist, cultural critic.

Obama, Barack (1961 -) American lawyer, politician, lawyer, US president 2009 to 2017.

Ogunlaru, Rasheed (1970 -) British author, coach, motivational speaker.

Osgood, Charles (1933 -) American radio and television commentator, writer and musician.

Picasso, Pablo (1881 - 1973) Spanish painter.

Pritchard, Michael (1949 -) American comedian, youth counsellor.

Player, Gary (1935 -) South African golfer.

Pope, Alexander (1688 - 1744) English poet, writer.

Robbins, Anthony (1960 -) American author, coach, speaker, philanthropist.

Rohn, Jim (1930 - 2009) American entrepreneur, author, motivational speaker.

Roosevelt, Eleanor (1884 - 1962) American diplomat, activist.

Ross, Allison (1972 -) South African vibrational alignment mentor, author.

Ross, Skip (1939 -2021) American business executive, theologian, speaker.

Rourke, Mickey (1952 -) American actor.

Rowling, Joanne K (1965 -) British author, philanthropist.

Rudd, Richard (1967 -) British teacher, mystic, author.

Rumi, Jalāl ad-Dīn Mohammad (1207 - 1273) Persian poet, theologian.

Sagan, Francoise (1935 - 2004) French playwright, novelist.

Sandberg, Sheryl (1969 -) American business executive, philanthropist, founder of Lean In.

Schuller, Robert (1926 - 2015) American pastor, evangelical speaker, author.

Schweitzer, Albert (1875 - 1965) Alsatian polymath.

Sealth, Chief Seattle (1780 - 1866) American Indian Duwamish) and Suquamish chief.

Seneca (the younger) Lucius Annaeus (Date unknown - 65AD) Roman philosopher statesman, dramatist.

Shakespeare, William (1564 - 1616) English playwright, poet.

Sharma, Robin (1964 -) Canadian author, speaker.

Shaw, George Bernard (1856 - 1950) Anglo-Irish playwright, political activist.

Sheehy, Gail (1936 - 2020) American journalist, author.

Sidey, Hugh (1927 - 2005) American journalist, author.

Sinek, Simon (1973 -) American author, motivational speaker.

Spence, Gerry (1929 -) American trial lawyer.

Stone, W Clement (1902 - 2002) American businessman, philanthropist, author.

Stravinsky, Igor (1882 - 1971) Russian composer.

Sunim, Haemin, (1973 -) South Korean Buddhist teacher, writer

Thackeray, William Makepeace (1811 - 1863) British author, illustrator.

Thoreau, Henry David (1817 - 1862) American writer, philosopher.

Toffler, Alvin (1928 - 2016) American futurist writer, businessman.

Tolstoy, Leo (1828 - 1910) Russian writer.

Tracy, Brian (1944 -) Canadian author, speaker.

Tzu, Chuang (c. 369 BC - c. 286 BC) Chinese philosopher and author.

Tzu, Lao (571 BC - Date unknown) Chinese philosopher, author of the Tao te Ching.

Vadlamani, Sonia (1986 -) Indian nutrition fitness, wellbeing consultant.

Van Gogh, Vincent (1853 - 1890) Dutch artist.

Washington, Denzel (1954 -) American actor, producer director.

Welker, Glenn H (1971 - 2005), American IT expert, researcher, writer.

Wilde, Oscar (1854 - 1900) Irish poet, playwright.

Windsor, Elizabeth II (1926 - 2022) Queen and Head of Commonwealth from1952 to 2022.

Witko, Thasunke, Crazy Horse (c. 1840 - 1877) Native American Lakota war leader.

Wonder, Stevie (1950 -) American singer, songwriter.

Ziglar, Zig (1926 - 2012) American author, motivational speaker.

Acknowledgements

My heartfelt thanks to:

All the **loved ones, friends and strangers** who have shared their *'treasures'* with me over the years.

The **Nottingham YES Group and Sam Pearce** whose session in April 2020 spurred me into action.

Alexander Inchbald and his Masterpiece community who encouraged and believed in me.

Ladey Adey for patiently guiding me through the birthing of this book.

Abbirose Adey for her skill with graphics and layout.

Stuart Davenall and **Alex Gaywood** for their insightful beta reading.

Doreen Hall and **Nola Smith** for their beautiful artwork and illustrations.

Jo Welch for patiently and lovingly capturing my essence.

243

About the Author

Sue Daly is a professional trainer and coach, with a fervent belief in the importance of clear and honest communication – with yourself and others – to create authentic and enduring relationships. She works holistically and intuitively, supporting people to recognise, embrace and live their full potential.

She lives in Nottinghamshire with her husband Terry, and their son Nicholas lives nearby.

Among Sue's interests are health, nature, gardening, walking, yoga and reading.

Contact Sue:

Website: www.sue-daly.com

LinkedIn: linkedin.com/in/suedaly

Please leave a review on Amazon for Sue.

Index

247

Your Favourite Quotes

I hope you enjoy gathering together your own quotations on the following blank pages, as I have done in various notebooks and scrapbooks over the years.

Several people have already said that they would like to contribute their own favourites if I were considering compiling another book, so if this is of interest to you please contact me to talk further.

Sue Daly

Lightning Source UK Ltd.
Milton Keynes UK
UKHW050238020323
417866UK00009B/132